Collins

Primary Social Studies for Antigua and Barbuda

WORKBOOK
GRADE 5

Anthea S Thomas

William Collins' dream of knowledge for all began with the publication of his first book in 1819.
A self-educated mill worker, he not only enriched millions of lives, but also founded a flourishing publishing house. Today, staying true to this spirit, Collins books are packed with inspiration, innovation and practical expertise. They place you at the centre of a world of possibility and give you exactly what you need to explore it.

Collins. Freedom to teach.

Published by Collins
An imprint of HarperCollins*Publishers*
The News Building
1 London Bridge Street
London
SE1 9GF

HarperCollins Publishers
Macken House, 39/40 Mayor Street Upper,
Dublin 1, D01 C9W8, Ireland

Browse the complete Collins catalogue at
www.collins.co.uk

10 9 8 7

ISBN 978-0-00-832497-1

British Library Cataloguing-in-Publication Data
A catalogue record for this publication is available from the British Library.

Author: Anthea S. Thomas
Commissioning editor: Elaine Higgleton
Development editor: Bruce Nicholson
In-house editors: Caroline Green, Alexandra Wells, Holly Woolnough
Copy editor: Sue Chapple
Proofreader: Jan Schubert
Answer checker: Hugh Hillyard-Parker
Cover designers: Kevin Robbins and Gordon MacGilp
Cover image: Imaginarybo/Shutterstock
Typesetter: QBS
Illustrators: QBS and Ann Paganuzzi
Production controller: Sarah Burke
Printed and Bound in the UK by Ashford Colour Press Ltd

Answers available at www.collins.co.uk/Caribbean

Acknowledgements

p20 Rodney Legall/Alamy Stock Photo; p21 NIKS ADS/Shutterstock.

Contents

1 Reading maps

Student's Book pages 5–16

1 Read pages 5–7 in the Student's Book. Use words from the box to fill in the blank spaces in the text below.

compass   relief   symbols   pictorial   features

topographical   cities   weather   elevation   roads

map   language

A _____ is a drawing that shows the location of various

_____ on the Earth's surface. It is a _____

representation of part of the Earth's surface.

Map reading is the ability to understand the _____ used

on maps, that is, to be able to recognise the _____ used, to

describe a piece of country and to interpret what the various features shown

indicate.

There are different types of maps that give different types of information.

Some common ones include _____ maps, which tell us about

weather conditions and forecasts, and _____ maps which give

us information on the physical features of a country.

_____ maps are the most useful and show a lot of information

such as _____, railways, boundaries and vegetation.

Maps use symbols to represent real things. Dots of varying sizes are

used for _____ and colours are used to represent

_____.

A _____ on a map helps us to give the direction of features or

places shown.

2 Read page 7 in the Student's Book. Add the missing points on the compass.

3 Measure the distances represented by these lines, using the scale shown.

0   10   20 kilometres

4 Read pages 10–13 in the Student's Book. Use words from the box to fill in the blank spaces in the text below.

zones	north	coordinate	Equator	longitude
degrees	latitude	west	meridians	location
parallels	Circle	time	Greenwich	Cancer	poles

Lines of _____ run from east to _____

on a map or globe. They are also known as _____

because they never meet. They help us to locate places north or

south of the _____. Lines of latitude are measured in

_____ north or south. The main line of latitude is the Equator.

Other special lines of latitude include the Tropic of _____, the

Tropic of Capricorn and the Arctic _____.

Lines of _____ run from _____ to south on a

map or globe. They are also called _____. The main line of

longitude is called the Prime Meridian or the _____ Meridian.

Lines of longitude are measured in degrees east or west. They meet at the

_____.

Lines of longitude are used to calculate _____, with the Earth

divided into 24 time _____.

A _____ is formed when a line of latitude meets a line of

longitude. They give us the exact _____ of places.

5 Find the words related to Unit I below in the wordsearch.

X	T	M	G	S	H	E	W	D	B	S	C	I	A	E
Y	O	O	C	N	R	T	I	A	Y	S	O	P	E	Y
C	S	A	P	U	I	R	R	F	I	A	O	F	R	V
N	L	M	S	O	E	D	D	A	N	P	R	L	I	F
E	E	A	R	C	G	I	A	O	E	M	D	E	A	L
R	E	T	T	O	S	R	I	E	O	O	I	D	L	O
M	E	I	Z	T	F	T	A	I	R	C	N	U	G	C
H	O	L	A	E	A	D	T	P	U	A	A	T	S	A
N	N	N	I	V	Q	A	N	L	H	E	T	I	E	T
L	C	G	E	E	R	U	N	A	G	I	E	G	J	I
E	B	L	G	O	F	M	A	P	L	W	C	N	N	O
R	E	P	R	E	S	E	N	T	A	T	I	O	N	N
L	A	T	I	T	U	D	E	K	O	Y	V	L	W	Y
L	A	I	R	O	T	C	I	P	T	R	H	B	V	T
G	D	Y	B	S	L	O	B	M	Y	S	N	Y	Q	F

aerial   compass   coordinate   direction   distance

earth   elevation   equator   landforms   latitude

location   longitude   map   measure   pictorial

ratio   reading   relief   representation   scale

symbols   topographic

6 Complete the crossword. All the words relate to Unit 1 in the Student's Book.

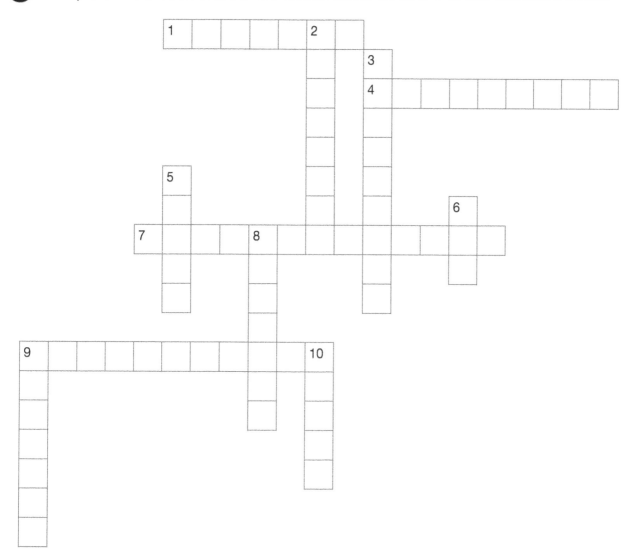

Across

1. Used to represent features on a map (6)
4. Lines running from north to south (9)
7. Main line of longitude (5, 8)
9. Formed where a line of latitude and a line of longitude meets (11)

Down

2. Lines running from east to west (8)
3. The height of the land (9)
5. A point on the compass (5)
6. A drawing of features on the Earth's surface (3)
8. Main line of latitude (7)
9. Used to give directions (7)
10. Used to measure distance on a map (5)

7 Read pages 13 and 14 in the Student's Book. Unscramble these words and write the correct letters in the spaces.

a crafia   A _ _ _ _ _

b rsuliaata   A _ _ _ _ _ _ _ _

c aisa   A _ _ _

d eouepr   E _ _ _ _ _

e hceinratmrao   N _ _ _ _   _ _ _ _ _ _ _

f tireomahaucs   S _ _ _ _   _ _ _ _ _ _ _

g aaacntrtci   A _ _ _ _ _ _ _ _ _

h fcapcaencoii   P _ _ _ _ _ _ _ _ _

i anaoinndcei   I _ _ _ _ _   _ _ _ _ _

j eceotunsnhroa   S _ _ _ _ _ _ _ _ _ _ _

k ciontceraac   A _ _ _ _ _ _ _ _ _

l ctinlotcaeana   A _ _ _ _ _ _ _   _ _ _ _ _

8 Draw a line to match each word on the left with its meaning on the right. You can use the internet to help if needed.

a isthmus

b oceans

c island

d strait

e peninsula

f continents

g valley

h mountain

i gulf

j plain

i a piece of land completely surrounded by water

ii a piece of land jutting out to sea and surrounded by water on three sides

iii a narrow strip of land joining two larger pieces of land together

iv large landmasses on the Earth's surface

v the largest bodies of water on the Earth's surface.

vi a narrow stretch of water between two land areas.

vii a part of a sea or ocean partly enclosed by land

viii a flat area of grassland

ix a stretch of low land between two areas of high land

x a very high piece of land with steep sides

9 Write the coordinates of the places A-E shown below

A _____

B _____

C _____

D _____

E _____

2 Weather and climate

Student's Book pages 17–26

1 Read pages 17–19 in the Student's Book. Use words from the box to fill in the blank spaces in the sentences below.

> weather   day   instruments   climate   wind   meteorologists
>
> V. C. Bird International Airport   temperature   cloudiness

a   The condition of the atmosphere over a short period of time is called the

   _____.

   It changes every _____.

b   The weather conditions over a long period of time tell us about the

   _____.

c   Special people called _____ collect information on

   a daily basis to tell us what the weather will be like.

d   The meteorological office in Antigua is located at the

   _____.

e   In order to tell us what the weather will be like, the weather

   forecaster looks at _____, rainfall,

   humidity, _____speed,

   _____ and visibility.

f   Special _____ are used to collect information

   about the weather.

2 Draw lines to link the weather features on the left with their definition on the right.

a	wind direction	**i**	how far one can see ahead
b	air pressure	**ii**	the amount of moisture in the air
c	visibility	**iii**	how hot or cold the air around us is
d	humidity	**iv**	how fast the wind is blowing
e	temperature	**v**	the direction in which the wind is blowing
f	windspeed	**vi**	the water that falls from the sky
g	rainfall	**vii**	the force exerted by the air

3 Use words from the box to fill the blank spaces in the sentences below.

> **thermometer**   **anemometer**   **rain gauge**
>
> **wind vane**   **barometer**

a A _____ is used to measure temperature.

b A _____ is used to measure the amount

of rainfall.

c A _____ is used to tell wind direction of the wind.

d An _____ is used to measure windspeed.

e A _____ is used to measure air pressure.

4 Unscramble the words, then match each one to the terms on the right.

a teoeethrmmr _____

b nair gaegu _____

c mreetabro _____

d emoeenmatr _____

e dinw aenv _____

i   air pressure

ii   temperature

iii wind speed

iv wind direction

v   rainfall

5 List and briefly explain the main factors that determine the type of climate a country has.

_____

_____

_____

_____

_____

_____

_____

_____

_____

6 Read page 20 in the Student's Book. Complete the diagram to show the characteristics of a tropical marine climate.

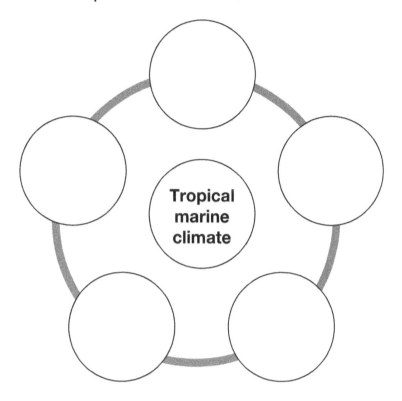

Tropical marine climate

7 Circle the correct word or words to complete each of these sentences.

a A person who tells us what the weather will be like is a

geologist archaeologist scientist meteorologist

b Visibility is …

how far ahead one can see

how many animals one can see

how many buildings one can see

how much rain one can see

c A thermometer is used to measure …

rainfall temperature wind direction air pressure

d All of the following are caused by changes in the weather except …

a landslide a flood a hurricane a volcanic eruption

8 Find the words related to Unit 2 below in the wordsearch.

Z	T	K	N	R	S	W	Q	W	W	A	W	T	R	B
S	C	E	A	A	E	U	I	E	T	Q	S	H	I	A
H	S	I	M	A	N	N	N	M	Q	I	H	E	T	R
T	N	E	T	P	D	E	O	N	G	N	U	R	E	O
Y	R	H	N	S	E	S	M	O	Y	Y	M	M	M	M
G	E	O	P	I	P	R	L	O	D	E	I	O	S	E
R	K	E	P	H	D	O	A	U	M	I	D	M	R	T
R	E	I	E	R	R	U	O	T	R	E	I	E	G	E
D	J	R	E	O	I	L	O	I	U	U	T	T	Y	R
G	E	D	E	V	C	A	I	L	S	R	Y	E	S	W
S	A	T	E	L	L	I	T	E	C	R	E	R	R	I
Q	E	W	I	N	D	D	I	R	E	C	T	I	O	N
M	Y	T	I	L	I	B	I	S	I	V	S	C	D	D
F	O	R	E	C	A	S	T	E	R	T	Z	X	D	Y
E	G	U	A	G	N	I	A	R	B	R	E	E	Z	Y

---

airport   anemometer   atmosphere   barometer

breezy   cloudiness   cloudy   forecaster

humidity   meteorologist   rain gauge   rainy

satellite   sunny   temperature   thermometer

visibility   weather   wind direction

windspeed   windy

3 Customs and culture

Student's Book pages 27–47

1 Find the words related to customs and culture in the wordsearch.

E	Q	T	B	O	M	D	E	Q	B	N	Z	N	X	N	M	T	D	H	G
O	T	R	S	D	J	N	G	L	S	T	Y	A	W	P	C	B	M	P	R
S	R	A	O	G	A	I	W	U	G	J	A	T	S	S	S	R	G	V	D
G	I	D	M	I	J	N	S	B	P	O	C	Q	E	C	K	R	H	S	M
E	X	I	M	I	R	C	E	T	I	M	B	L	A	I	G	L	X	K	N
V	C	T	L	W	L	L	B	Q	I	V	U	W	N	S	C	A	A	R	D
G	B	I	D	B	I	C	T	R	S	R	B	V	N	U	B	O	L	Q	L
P	E	O	T	E	E	I	Q	F	D	M	K	M	L	M	S	Y	S	X	P
L	H	N	F	C	R	H	I	D	E	L	N	T	C	P	J	P	P	G	J
V	A	S	E	Q	A	E	M	X	X	S	U	J	Z	T	B	Y	S	F	Y
U	V	N	F	R	W	R	B	S	O	R	R	O	P	A	E	U	D	G	K
O	I	O	G	N	A	I	P	C	E	E	Q	N	V	W	U	K	G	R	Q
C	O	R	H	U	P	T	X	L	I	N	I	Q	P	O	Q	P	H	Z	K
D	U	M	L	P	A	A	I	R	M	Y	H	L	B	S	L	S	M	F	Z
M	R	S	E	D	P	G	E	O	V	N	M	N	C	Z	H	S	Z	F	G
C	H	G	T	O	I	E	E	C	N	A	D	D	I	R	T	J	M	D	I
J	T	W	H	O	Q	C	A	Y	A	N	F	D	G	L	U	R	D	N	N
T	K	R	N	O	M	M	V	O	P	H	Q	N	O	D	G	P	D	J	Y
U	A	O	I	E	U	S	Z	W	Y	T	O	H	L	F	R	O	V	R	U
A	M	A	C	A	S	J	K	U	B	T	G	M	K	X	T	N	Y	J	F

> behaviour   beliefs   climate   culture   customs
> dance   ethnic   food   generation   heritage   language
> music   norms   practice   religion   rules   society   traditions

2 Complete the crossword. All the words relate to Unit 3 in the Student's Book.

Across

4. Where the languages spoken in the Caribbean came from (6)
6. Celebrating the birth of Jesus Christ (9)
8. Grandsons of the prophet Mohammed (6)
9. Dance and drum originated from here (6)
11. Festival of Lights (6)

Down

1. Way of life of a group of people (7)
2. A showcase of Caribbean arts (9)
3. Lasting about 30 years (10)
5. Colour of the Antiguan pineapple (5)
6. Celebration of emancipation (8)
7. An Indian religion (8)
10. Acceptable practices of a community (7)

3 Use words from the box to fill the gaps in the sentences below.

| cultural heritage culture tradition customs folklore |

a _____ is many aspects of the way of life of a group of people.

b _____ are an accepted practice of a community or a group

of people.

c A _____ is a practice, custom or story that is memorised and

passed down from generation to generation.

d The traditional beliefs, myths, stories, sayings and practices in a culture

can be called its _____.

e In Antigua and Barbuda, our rich culture depends on our people with

their different backgrounds and experiences. They have given us our

_____.

4 Look at the picture below and then answer the questions.

a What is the name of the festival shown in the picture?

_____

b What is the significance of the festival?

_____

_____

_____

c Name two countries where this festival is celebrated.

_____

_____

d Name two activities that take place during the festival.

_____

_____

5 Look at this picture and then answer the questions.

a What is the name of the festival shown in the picture?

_____

b What is the significance of the festival?

_____

_____

_____

c Name two countries where this festival is celebrated.

_____

_____

d Name two activities that take place during the festival.

_____

_____

6 Give a short explanation of the significance of each festival listed below.

a Hosay

_____

_____

b Christmas

_____

_____

c Diwali

_____

_____

d Crop Over

_____

_____

7 Complete the sentences with the correct word from the box.

> beliefs   five   **Rastafarianism**   **Judaism**
>
> **Christianity**   **Hinduism**   social system   **Islam**

Religion is a system of _____ that helps people make sense

of the world. There are _____ main religions in the Caribbean

today.

_____ is the major religion of the Caribbean. It is divided into

several denominations.

_____ is a highly-organised _____ and way of

life, as well as a religion.

_____ refers is the religion practised by Muslims.

_____ is the religion of the Jewish people. It includes both a

world view and a way of life.

_____ is a movement of black people who believe that Africa

was the birthplace of mankind.

8 Read pages 41–43 in the Student's Book. Then write the music and food words next to the island they are associated with.

> **calypso**　**flying fish**　**salsa**　**reggae**　**saltfish**　**benna**
>
> **fungee and pepperpot**　**ropa vieja**　**string band**
>
> **stewed saltfish**　**ackee**

a Jamaica _____

b Cuba _____

c St. Kitts and Nevis _____

d Antigua and Barbuda _____

e Barbados _____

9 Give three reasons for the changes that have occurred in Caribbean culture over the years.

_____

_____

_____

_____

_____

10 A community of people from various ethnic backgrounds decide to have a food fair, with foods from various Caribbean countries. Give two possible benefits of this activity to the community.

_____

_____

_____

_____

_____

11 Answer these questions. You can use the internet to help you if necessary.

a Define the term 'customs'.

_____

_____

b Apart from the family, name two social groups that can encourage the teaching of local customs and culture.

_____

_____

c Antigua and Barbuda has an annual Independence Food Fair. Name one local food that can be included in this fair.

_____

_____

d Here are two festivals in the Caribbean: Crop Over, John Canoe. Can you add three more to the list?

_____

_____

_____

e Chose one of the festivals that you have added to the list and state two activities that usually take place during the festival.

_____

_____

f Suggest one way citizens of Antigua and Barbuda can keep their culture alive.

_____

_____

g Steel pan is part of the culture of Antigua and Barbuda. What are your views about playing steel pan in church?

_____

_____

12 Write the meaning of each of the following local sayings. You can use the internet to help you if necessary.

a Waste not want not.

_____

_____

b A still tongue keeps a wise head.

_____

_____

c Every dog have dey day.

_____

_____

d Cockroach na hab no right inna fowl house.

_____

_____

e Give Jack e jacket.

_____

_____

f You kill me dog, me kill you cat.

_____

_____

g You do more barking dan wa bitin.

_____

_____

13 Using what you have read in the Student's Book, and from your own research among family members and friends, explain how the culture in Antigua and Barbuda today is different from that of a generation ago.

_____

_____

_____

_____

_____

_____

_____

_____

4 Population of Antigua and Barbuda

Student's Book pages 48–57

1 Use words from the box to fill in the gaps in the text below.

> wars   migration   disasters   emigrants
>
> immigrants   life

The movement of people from place to place is called _____.

People move for different reasons, but the most popular reason is that they

are in search of a better way of _____. Other reasons why

people migrate include to study, to escape from _____ and to

avoid natural _____.

People who leave their native country and go to live in another country are

called _____.

People who come to live in our country from another country are called

_____.

2 Complete the crossword. All the answers relate to migration and are from Unit 4 in the Student's Book.

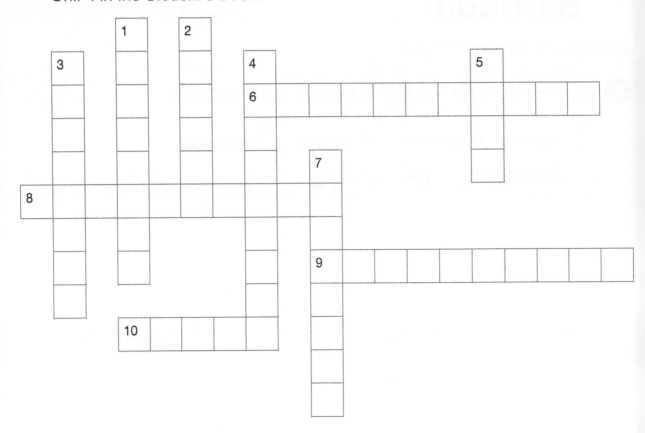

Across

6. Coming to live in a country that is not your own (11)

8. The removal of important skills from a country (5, 5)

9. Leaving one country to live in another (10)

10. Migration where someone follows friends or family (5)

Down

1. Differences in ideas can lead to this (8)

2. Migration that is caused by disasters and wars (6)

3. Migration which involves moving from your country of birth to another country (8)

4. The movement of people from place to place (9)

5. Migration done in a series of small moves (4)

7. Migration within one's own country (8)

3 Draw lines to link each term on the left with its correct definition on the right.

a external migration

b step migration

c forced migration

d internal migration

e chain migration

i the movement of people within their own country

ii the movement of people caused by a disaster or by war

iii following the movements of others, usually family or friends

iv a series of small movements from one place to another

v the movement of people from their country of birth to another country

4 Fill in the bubbles with reasons why people might migrate to Antigua and Barbuda.

5 Fill in the table to show the push and pull factors of migration. Use the information from the box below.

unemployment   overpopulation

good health care and education systems   discrimination

strong economic growth   natural disaster   poor health care

war or oppression   poverty/low wages   proper rights

rights and freedom   crime   low cost of living

compulsory military service   corruption   high taxes

famine   demand for labour   high wages

generous welfare benefits   technology

family and friends/networks   law and order

Push factors	Pull factors

6 Complete the diagrams to show the possible effects of immigration and emigration on countries.

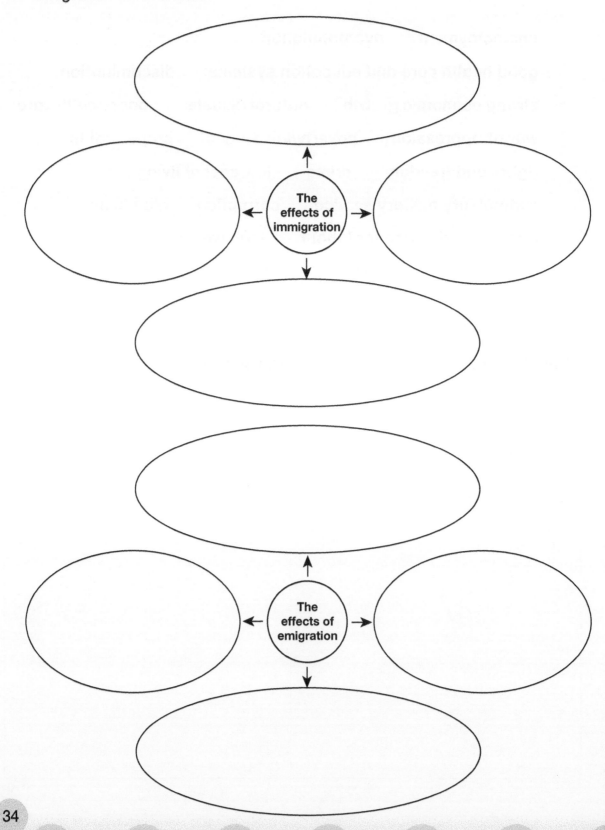

7 Suggest some strategies that the government of Antigua and Barbuda might use to discourage highly-skilled people from migrating.

_____

_____

_____

_____

_____

_____

_____

_____

_____

_____

_____

_____

8 Explain some of the possible effects of migration on families.

_____

_____

_____

_____

_____

_____

_____

_____

_____

_____

9 Circle the correct answer for each of the following.

   a People who are forced to leave their homes are called ...

   nomads   refugees   wanderers   mummies

   b All of the following are possible effects of immigration except ...

   population increase   brain drain   overcrowding   conflicts

   c The emigration of skilled people from a country is referred to as ...

   under population   overcrowding   brain drain   population

   d The check on the population of Antigua and Barbuda that is carried out every 10 years is called the ...

   distribution   census   ethnic balance   birth rate

10 Create a questionnaire of 10 questions that can be used to gather information from the census.

_____

_____

_____

_____

_____

_____

_____

_____

11 Give as many reasons as you can to explain why the census is important to Antigua and Barbuda.

_____

_____

_____

_____

_____

_____

_____

_____

12 Find the words related to migration below in the wordsearch.

M	A	T	L	F	H	X	X	B	S	N	Z	O	L	Z
S	I	W	N	E	O	F	U	E	F	Y	I	E	T	B
R	F	G	A	E	E	R	E	T	O	K	E	A	D	R
A	O	L	R	L	M	M	C	T	G	W	E	O	R	A
W	T	Z	J	A	I	E	F	E	L	Q	G	A	W	B
H	D	V	Q	G	T	I	V	R	D	I	U	Z	D	Q
C	P	Q	R	G	Z	I	A	O	J	M	F	L	Q	P
H	X	A	O	C	F	H	O	I	M	M	E	D	G	U
A	N	U	H	V	X	L	O	N	Z	I	R	B	L	J
T	R	E	T	S	A	S	I	D	N	G	U	M	B	L
H	P	B	P	C	A	N	A	T	U	R	A	L	E	P
S	L	L	I	K	S	Z	I	T	K	A	G	X	E	Z
F	E	D	I	Q	W	L	T	C	V	N	V	J	H	E
I	E	J	Z	H	N	L	B	L	B	T	W	S	Y	T
M	R	I	M	M	I	G	R	A	T	I	O	N	Z	G

better	brain	disaster	emigrant	forced	health

immigrant   immigration   medical   migration   movement

natural   refugee   skills   wars

13 Read pages 52–54 in the Student's Book. Use words from the box to fill in the blank spaces in the sentences below.

population   housing   census   education

ten   population density   migration   gender

a The _____ refers to the total number of people living in the country.

b A _____ is a count of the population of a country.

c _____ _____ is the term given to the analysis of how many people live in different parts of the country.

d A census is conducted every _____ years.

e One of the factors affecting the size and structure of a population is _____.

f A census tells the government how many people live there, their _____ and age, their level of _____, the work they do and the type of _____ they live in.

14 Complete the crossword. All the answers relate to population and migration and are from Unit 4 in the Student's Book.

Across

4. Used to give the official count of the population of a country (6)
6. How well populated an area is (7)
7. Factors that cause people to leave a country (4)
8. The movement of people from place to place (9)

Down

1. An area with few people living there is said to be .... populated (8)
2. A high .... rate may cause the population to increase (5)
3. Male or female (6)
5. This type of migration involves a series of moves (4)

15 Read page 53 in the Student's Book. Make a note of the factors affecting population size.

Population increase

_____

_____

_____

_____

_____

_____

_____

Population decrease

_____

_____

_____

_____

_____

_____

_____

16 In your own words, describe the main characteristics of population.

17 Complete the diagram to show the factors that affect population density and explain what each means.

```
                    ┌──────────────┐
                    │              │
                    │              │
                    └──────┬───────┘
                           │
                           ▼
┌──────────────┐      ╭─────────╮      ┌──────────────┐
│              │ ───▶ │Population│ ◀─── │              │
│              │      │ density  │      │              │
└──────────────┘      ╰─────────╯      └──────────────┘
                       ▲         ▲
┌──────────────┐      │         │      ┌──────────────┐
│              │ ─────╯         ╰───── │              │
│              │                       │              │
└──────────────┘                       └──────────────┘
```

_____

_____

_____

_____

_____

_____

_____

_____

_____

18 Look at the questions about population. Circle the correct answer.

a) The population of a country is the …

number of people in a shop.

number of people living in a particular place on a particular date.

number of people at the football match

number of people attending school

b) A population census is held every _____ years.

10

12

14

16

c) All of the following can cause the population to increase except …

immigration

birth

death

alien invasion

19 Find the words related to population in the word search puzzle.

G	P	U	Z	L	O	P	R	E	I	R	M	V	O	E
L	H	O	B	C	S	R	U	Y	O	K	I	E	K	E
Z	S	Z	P	H	Z	A	M	T	S	I	G	F	V	A
D	V	F	T	U	L	K	A	V	U	A	R	U	D	H
V	Z	R	F	S	L	R	Y	Z	S	K	A	L	P	X
M	I	D	D	N	E	A	V	L	N	O	T	P	E	E
B	Z	I	L	M	E	Q	T	S	E	N	I	P	S	H
A	Z	G	U	U	I	W	P	I	C	S	O	Q	Z	Z
I	Z	N	V	E	U	A	W	V	O	M	N	E	W	P
D	E	M	O	G	R	A	P	H	Y	N	B	E	Y	E
W	W	B	Q	S	D	E	A	T	H	S	N	H	D	D
U	Z	X	E	B	P	B	U	U	V	L	M	F	G	H
W	P	L	T	G	W	Y	S	K	O	X	X	V	M	R
G	Y	C	F	I	C	I	F	H	S	E	W	D	Y	J

births   census   deaths   demography   densely

enumerator   migration   population   sparsely

5 Production of goods

Student's Book pages 58–67

1 Find the words related to the production of goods, listed below, in the wordsearch.

I	N	U	O	T	R	G	F	E	B	M	M	Y	T	L
G	N	J	N	S	R	A	O	A	K	R	A	R	R	O
Z	K	T	T	O	C	O	S	O	A	F	N	E	O	C
I	H	R	E	T	I	I	P	W	D	S	U	N	P	A
N	M	B	O	R	C	T	M	M	E	S	F	I	X	L
B	K	R	K	Q	N	A	C	I	I	R	A	H	E	B
F	Y	D	R	A	T	A	R	U	X	P	C	C	R	A
T	R	A	D	E	T	T	T	M	D	X	T	A	E	B
C	U	R	R	E	N	C	Y	I	Z	O	U	M	G	W
M	F	I	Y	U	W	Z	L	J	O	Q	R	A	I	S
Y	A	H	O	G	R	D	U	W	V	N	E	P	O	A
L	D	C	Y	F	S	I	T	A	S	X	A	S	N	P
S	C	I	N	O	R	T	C	E	L	E	G	L	A	S
G	L	F	Z	U	K	C	F	L	J	P	X	C	L	R
F	W	S	D	E	E	N	E	U	A	C	V	D	L	O

basic	countries	currency	electronics	export

factory	goods	import	international	local

machinery	manufacture	needs	production

raw material	regional	satisfy	trade

2 Use words from the box to fill in the gaps in the sentences below.

quaternary	tertiary	secondary	four	factories	sea
manufacturing	primary	land	industry	service	

a Any activity that earns money is called an _____.

b There are _____ types of industry.

c In a _____ industry, the workers take things from the

_____ and the _____.

d In a _____ industry, the workers take the things from the land

and sea and make them into something useful.

e In a _____ or _____ industry, the workers provide

services to the general population and to businesses.

f In a _____ industry, the workers provide knowledge and skills,

such as in scientific research and with computers.

g Products are produced in _____ on a large scale using

machinery. This is called _____.

3 Find the words related to industry in the wordsearch.

L	A	U	B	X	D	X	J	D	Z	C	C	L	D	R	T	I	B	L	P
G	M	Z	Y	Y	R	Y	O	Y	N	Y	I	F	M	A	T	Z	O	M	S
H	C	W	V	T	J	E	C	C	R	R	Z	G	X	I	I	X	X	L	C
K	T	O	U	R	I	S	M	Y	R	A	M	I	R	P	Z	H	F	F	J
D	H	L	J	O	F	V	T	A	D	N	D	Y	W	E	D	A	R	T	E
P	X	C	K	P	G	M	I	N	E	R	S	N	E	J	M	E	Z	K	Q
Z	R	O	R	M	X	L	H	T	I	E	Q	L	O	P	H	R	T	E	V
U	D	S	J	I	R	X	Z	V	C	T	B	D	J	C	M	V	A	Z	P
W	P	J	F	I	S	H	E	R	M	A	N	N	A	M	E	R	I	F	D
J	O	Q	O	A	O	R	U	D	W	U	A	E	P	X	O	S	Z	K	S
X	B	R	W	B	H	O	T	E	L	Q	T	I	P	J	E	K	K	G	H
T	H	Y	K	N	S	P	N	P	W	M	U	O	S	K	A	H	Q	V	O
P	H	N	R	E	T	E	R	T	I	A	R	Y	V	C	V	U	W	G	V
U	W	C	R	X	R	Z	I	B	K	T	A	Q	I	O	O	H	F	J	S
E	M	A	W	V	Q	S	P	E	W	S	L	W	D	I	V	I	O	X	Y

activity   export   farmer   fireman   fisherman   hotel

import   jobs   miner   natural   primary   quaternary

renewable   resources   secondary   taxi driver   teacher

tertiary   tourism   trade   workers

4 Complete the crossword. All the answers relate to industry and are from Unit 5 in the Student's Book.

Across

5. An example of a primary industry (7)

7. Workers in this sector provide a service (8)

9. A worker in a hospital who provides a service (5)

10. Industry where workers make useful things from natural resources (9)

Down

1. Usually done in factories (13)

2. Anything that is useful (8)

3. An example of a worker in a quaternary industry (9)

4. An example of a secondary industry which involves building (11)

6. Industry where things are taken from the land and the sea (7)

8. An activity that earns money (8)

5 Decide which type of industry these jobs belong to. Write them in the table in the correct column.

mining   fishing   car production   clerical services

insurance services   banking   farming   construction

quarrying   scientific research

Primary	Secondary	Tertiary	Quaternary

6 Complete the diagram below by choosing from the list. Then give two further examples of each type of industry. You can use the internet to help if necessary.

> banking   sand mining   farming   sugar production
>
> nursing   soft drink production

```
                    ┌─────────────────┐
                    │    Types of     │
                    │   industries    │
                    └─────────────────┘
                             │
        ┌────────────────────┼────────────────────┐
   ┌─────────┐          ┌──────────┐          ┌──────────┐
   │ Primary │          │ Secondary│          │ Tertiary │
   └─────────┘          └──────────┘          └──────────┘
        │                    │                     │
   ┌─────────┐          ┌──────────┐          ┌──────────┐
   │         │          │          │          │          │
   │         │          │          │          │          │
   └─────────┘          └──────────┘          └──────────┘
        │                    │                     │
   ┌─────────┐          ┌──────────┐          ┌──────────┐
   │         │          │          │          │          │
   └─────────┘          └──────────┘          └──────────┘
```

7 Fill in the diagram with the correct examples from the box below for each type of industry. You can use the internet to help if necessary.

> thread   steel   corn   cloth   oil   leather
>
> camera   microwave   laptop   computer   dolls
>
> mobile phone   telephone   gold   oil refining
>
> paper   refrigerator

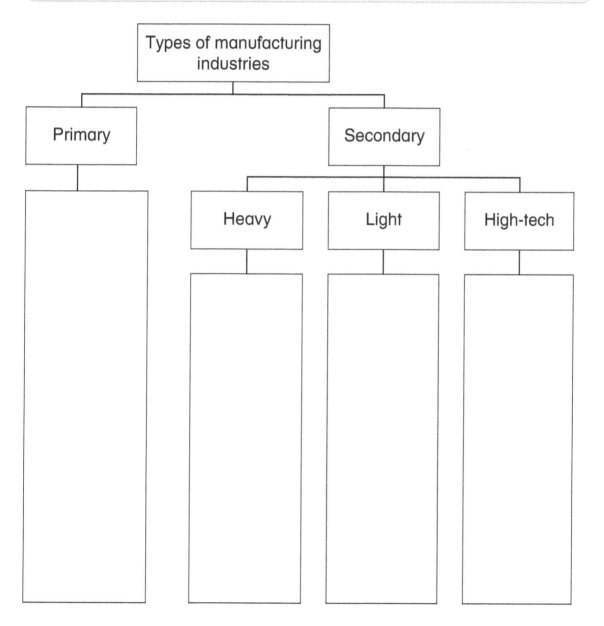

Types of manufacturing industries

Primary

Secondary

Heavy

Light

High-tech

8 Malcolm is a farmer who grows a lot of tomatoes. Last year, a large part of his crop of tomatoes was left to spoil. He decided that in order to reduce the waste of tomatoes in future that he was going to create a manufacturing business that would use them. What factors does Malcolm have to consider when deciding where to locate his manufacturing business?

_____

_____

_____

_____

_____

_____

_____

_____

_____

9 Jahmeka loves baking and she has been selling baked goods out of her home. However, it has become so popular that she has a large number of customers and needs to expand and create a proper retailing business. What factors should Jahmeka consider in choosing the location for her retailing business?

_____

_____

_____

_____

_____

_____

_____

_____

10 What are the factors that should be considered when moving a retail business home or abroad?

_____

_____

_____

_____

_____

_____

_____

_____

6 Distribution of goods

Student's Book pages 68–75

1 Draw a line to link each of these terms on the left with its correct definition on the right.

a	trading currency	**i**	To buy goods from another country
b	manufacturing	**ii**	The buying and selling of goods and services
c	cottage industry		
d	agro-industry	**iii**	A fast but expensive way of sending goods
e	import	**iv**	The selling of goods to other countries
f	air transport	**v**	Money used for trading
g	export	**vi**	Creation of goods in a home
h	trade	**vii**	The preservation and preparation of agricultural products.
		viii	To create a finished product from raw material

2 Make a list of some goods that are produced in Antigua and Barbuda and some that have to be imported.

Goods that can be obtained locally	Goods that must be imported

3 Complete the flow chart to show the production of something from raw material to finished product. You can make your own choice. You can use the internet to help if necessary.

```
┌─────────────────┐        ┌─────────────────┐
│                 │   →    │                 │
└─────────────────┘        └─────────────────┘
                                     ↓
┌─────────────────┐        ┌─────────────────┐
│                 │   ←    │                 │
└─────────────────┘        └─────────────────┘
        ↓
┌─────────────────┐        ┌─────────────────┐
│                 │   →    │                 │
└─────────────────┘        └─────────────────┘
```

4 Explain the different methods used to distribute goods.

_____

_____

_____

_____

_____

_____

_____

---

5 What problems can affect the distribution of goods? Describe them briefly.

---

6 How important are workers to the production and distribution of goods?

_____

_____

_____

_____

_____

_____

_____

_____

7 Tourism

Student's Book pages 76–92

1 Find the words related to tourism below in the wordsearch.

I	V	S	P	O	R	T	S	T	O	U	R	I	S	M	V
H	E	R	I	T	A	G	E	T	O	U	R	I	S	M	B
N	O	I	T	A	D	O	M	M	O	C	C	A	E	T	A
P	P	O	E	C	O	T	O	U	R	I	S	M	N	N	F
R	P	L	L	C	I	Q	R	T	V	A	X	Z	I	E	Z
G	Z	H	E	A	L	T	H	T	O	U	R	I	S	M	X
W	J	I	V	A	W	I	S	R	O	U	Y	L	U	E	B
W	O	H	A	M	S	X	M	E	E	U	R	C	B	V	I
Y	D	Y	R	N	J	U	P	A	M	G	R	I	C	O	Z
H	X	A	T	E	X	A	R	L	T	O	I	I	S	M	X
X	H	S	E	C	I	V	R	E	S	E	D	O	S	M	G
G	E	E	N	T	E	R	T	A	I	N	M	E	N	T	E
S	G	B	I	N	T	E	R	N	A	T	I	O	N	A	L
G	N	N	E	P	W	C	T	U	P	C	J	S	C	R	L
P	C	V	N	C	H	K	A	O	R	H	S	V	Z	Y	X
G	M	K	K	B	G	M	V	B	C	X	L	U	A	C	K

accommodation	business	climate	domestic
ecotourism	entertainment	health tourism	international
movement	pleasure	regional	services	sports tourism
tourism	heritage tourism	tourist	travel

2 Fill in the blank spaces with the correct words.

> **services**   **tourism**   **entertainment**   **activity**

_____ is the business _____ connected with

providing accommodation, _____ and _____ for

people who visit for pleasure.

3 Draw a line to link each term on the left with its correct definition on the right.

a ecotourism

b sports tourism

c health tourism

d culture and heritage tourism

i tourism with an interest in historical sites, celebrations, festivals, food and dancing, etc.

ii tourism with an interest in preserving the natural environment of a country

iii tourism where people can participate in or watch events taking place

iv tourism offering the best health care facilities available to cater to the needs of the sick

4 Say what type of tourist each of the following persons are. Choose from:

- domestic/local tourist
- regional tourist
- international tourist.

a Jack lives in All Saints, but he spent the weekend with his family in St. John's.

_____

b Sandra travelled from New York to visit her grandmother in Antigua.

_____

c Karen went to Barbuda for the Caribana and returned to Antigua on Monday evening.

_____

d Janet, who lives in Dominica, spent her summer vacation in Barbados.

_____

e A group of Antiguan cricketers travelled to Australia to play cricket.

_____

f The Antigua Pentecostal Crusaders went to a camp in Trinidad for ten days.

_____

g Former Prime Minister Hon. Baldwin Spencer went to a meeting in St. Kitts for the weekend.

_____

h Sean took the ferry from St. Kitts to Nevis to visit his uncle for the summer vacation.

_____

5 Match these terms with their correct definition.

a) tourist _____

b) international tourist _____

c) culture and heritage tourism _____

d) tourism _____

e) regional tourist _____

f) health tourism _____

g) sports tourism _____

h) ecotourism _____

i) domestic tourist _____

i) Creating an interest in historical sites, celebrations, festivals, food and dancing, etc.

ii) The business activity connected with providing accommodation, entertainment and services for people who travel for business or pleasure.

iii) A person who leaves his or her usual place of residence for 24 hours or more.

iv) A person who travels outside of his or her region.

v) Creating sporting events so that people can participate or watch them take place.

vi) A person who travels within his or her region.

vii) A person who travels within his or her own country.

viii) Creating the best health care facilities available to cater to the needs of the sick.

ix) Creating an interest in preserving the natural beauty of a country.

6 Use words from the box to fill the blank spaces in the sentences below.

> attractions   flora   physical   spectator   superb
>
> climate   springs   forests   fauna   celebrations

a   We have our warm _____ and many tourist

   _____. The climate in the Caribbean is

   _____ all year round, with the winter milder and more

   tolerable than in some countries.

b   There is plenty to see, with _____ features such as

   beaches, caves, reefs and _____.

c   There is plenty of _____ to see, such as beautiful flowers,

   trees and tropical _____.

d   There is plenty of _____ to see – birds, butterflies and

   other creatures.

e   Festivals, other _____ and sport, also pull individuals to the

   Caribbean as tourists.

f   There are many people who enjoy watching sports such as cricket,

   football, golf and many other _____ sports.

7 One way for countries to promote themselves as a tourist destination is by creating brochures and posters. In the space below create a poster which can be used to advertise Antigua and Barbuda as a major tourist destination.

8 Imagine that you are a singer, travelling around the world singing songs about what Antigua and Barbuda has to offer, to encourage tourists to visit your island. Compose a song that you could sing to help achieve your goal. It could be calypso, reggae, R&B, etc. Write the words in the box below.

9 Are they cultural, geographical or historical tourist attractions? Put each of these tourist attractions in the correct column.

> Pillars of Hercules   Betty's Hope   Devil's Bridge
>
> Frigate Bird Sanctuary   Sailing Week   Carnival
>
> Nelson's Dockyard   Fort James   Montpelier Sugar Factory
>
> Potworks Dam   Wallings rainforest

Cultural attractions	Geographical attractions	Historical attractions

10 Use words from the box to fill in the blank spaces in the sentences below.

> European   coastal   Modified American   packages
>
> Continental   guest house   place   apartment
>
> condominium   All Inclusive

a When tourists come to Antigua they need a _____ to stay.

b This can be a hotel, _____ _____,

_____ or _____.

c Many hotels in Antigua are located around the _____

areas.

d Many hotels have various _____ that they offer to the

tourists.

e In the _____ _____ Plan, the guest pays a

fixed rate for room, breakfast and dinner at the hotel (sometimes in other

restaurants too, on a 'dine around' plan.)

f In the _____ Plan, the hotel charges only for the room;

guests must arrange for their own meals, whether at the hotel or elsewhere

on the island.

g In the _____ Plan, a light breakfast (usually juice, coffee

and sweet roll) is included in the room charge.

h In _____ _____, the guest pays one hotel

fee which includes room, taxes, airport transfers, all meals, drinks, use of

hotel sports equipment and many extras.

11 Use Student's Book page 85 to answer these questions. You can also use the
internet to help with some of the questions.

a Areas where people can enter a country whether by air or sea are called

_____.

b There are _____ main ports of entry in Antigua and

Barbuda.

c The airport in Antigua is called _____.

d The airport in Barbuda is called _____.

e The port by which large goods are brought into the country is the

_____.

f The port where major cruise ships dock is the _____.

g Two other ports of entry are the _____ and

_____.

h The port that is known as the gateway to the eastern Caribbean is the

_____.

i Name five airlines that bring passengers to Antigua and Barbuda.

_____

_____

_____

_____

_____

j Name three cruise ships that bring passengers to Antigua.

_____

_____

_____

12 Write **A** for advantage on the line next to each statement if the statement is an advantage of tourism or **D** if the statement is a disadvantage of tourism.

a Tourism brings in a lot of money to the country. _____

b Some of the hotels are owned by foreigners so most of the profits from their operations go back to their own country. _____

c Tourism creates employment and provides a market for the local handicraft industries, as well as for local agricultural producers. _____

d Employment is seasonal and some hotels close their doors during off periods. _____

e Money from tourism plays a vital role in the country's economy. _____

f Tourists may be directly responsible for the damaging of the ecosystem, by collecting corals and seashells as souvenirs or buying them from the local people who have collected them for sale. _____

g The tourism industry is fragile. It may take years to develop but can disappear overnight. This may be because of outbreaks of disease, natural disasters, political unrest, etc. _____

h The government gains much-needed revenue from tourism through airport taxes, taxes on the hotel rooms, sales tax, entertainment tax, and restaurant and bar licences. _____

13 New technology has brought many improvements to the tourism industry. What are five ways in which technology can be used?

_____

_____

_____

_____

_____

_____

_____

_____

14 If you were a tourist making plans to travel, describe how you could use the internet to help.

_____

_____

_____

_____

8 Local and regional organisations

Student's Book pages 93–104

1 Use words from the box to fill in the blank spaces in the sentences below.

> church   school   regional   organisation   political
>
> local   international   National Office of Disaster Services

a A group of people working together to run something or achieve a common goal is called an _____.

b The Antigua and Barbuda Labour Party is a _____ organisation.

c An organisation may be _____, _____ or _____.

d _____ and _____ are examples of organisations that many people belong to.

e _____ is an organisation that help us in times of natural disasters.

2 Write the full names of these local organisations.

a ACB _____   e NODS _____

b CBH _____   f UPP _____

c DCA _____   g ABUT _____

d EAG _____   h APUA _____

3 Match each local organisation with the services it provides.

a Antigua and Barbuda Labour Party _____

b Antigua and Barbuda Trades and Labour Union _____

c Antigua and Barbuda Union of Teachers _____

d Antigua and Barbuda Workers' Union _____

e Antigua Commercial Bank _____

f Antigua Public Utilities Authority _____

g Central Board of Health _____

h Development Control Authority _____

i Environmental Awareness Group _____

j Kiwanis Club _____

k Leo Club _____

l National Solid Waste Management Authority _____

m National Office of Disaster Services _____

n Red Cross _____

i fights to protect the natural environment including plants and animals

ii a team of volunteers who strive to improve the world through service to children and the communities

iii a local bank owned by the people of Antigua and Barbuda; the bank provides services such as loans, savings and debit and credit cards

iv one of the major political parties in Antigua and Barbuda

v the junior branch of the Lions Club

vi responsible for ensuring that the people in the country are prepared for national disasters

vii fights for the rights of workers, especially for better working conditions and wages; it also fights for people who have been wrongfully dismissed from their jobs

viii fights for the rights of teachers, including better working conditions and salaries

ix the organisation looking after health services

x provides the people with electricity, telephone, water and internet services

xi fights for the rights of workers

xii makes sure all new building work is carried out to the necessary standard

xiii works to keep the environment is clean by collecting bulk waste and keeping the streets clean

xiv a volunteer organisation that provides assistance to people in need, especially in times of disasters

4 Answer these questions on regional organisations in the Caribbean.

a African Union (AU)

i When was the AU formed (replacing the Organisation of African Unity)?

_____

ii What are the main aims of the AU?

_____

_____

_____

_____

_____

b Organization of American States (OAS)

　i　When was the OAS formed?

　　_____

　ii　What are the main aims of the OAS?

　　_____

　　_____

　　_____

　iii　Where is the headquarters of the OAS?

　　_____

　iv　How many countries are a part of the OAS?

　　_____

　v　Name five of the countries that make up the OAS.

　　_____

　　_____

　　_____

　　_____

　　_____

c United Nations (UN)

　i　When was the UN formed?

　　_____

　ii　What are the main aims of the UN?

　　_____

　　_____

　　_____

iii Where is the headquarters of the UN?

_____

iv Who is the current Secretary General of the UN?

_____

v How many countries are a part of the UN?

_____

vi Name five of the countries that make up the UN.

_____

_____

_____

_____

d CARICOM

   i When was CARICOM formed?

_____

   ii What are the main aims of CARICOM?

_____

_____

_____

   iii Where is the headquarters of CARICOM?

_____

   iv How many countries are a part of CARICOM?

_____

v Name five of the countries that make up CARICOM.

_____

_____

_____

_____

_____

e Organisation of Eastern Caribbean States (OECS)

   i When was the OECS formed?

_____

   ii What are the main aims of the OECS?

_____

_____

_____

   iii Where is the headquarters of the OECS?

_____

   iv Who is the Director General of the OECS?

_____

   v How many countries are a part of the OECS?

_____

   vi Name five of the countries that make up the OECS.

_____

_____

_____

5 Read the events being described below. Choose from the box the abbreviation of the best organisation to help and write it after each event.

> **CARDI   CDEMA   UN   IMF   WHO**

a The Caribbean has been hit by an outbreak of chicken pox. The governments can call on this organisation. _____

b Antigua is having trouble repaying its debts. The government can call on this organisation. _____

c A hurricane destroyed most of the country's buildings .The government can call on this organisation. _____

d There is a dispute between two countries. The governments can call on this organisation. _____

e There is a plant disease that is causing coconut trees to die. The government can call on this organisation. _____

6 Place the organisations listed below under the correct heading in the table.

OECS   APUA   UN   OAS   IMF   CDERA   UWI

CDB   UNESCO   WHO   CDEMA   CARIFESTA

CARICOM   AU   ACB

Local	Regional	International